THE GOLDEN COMPASS™

THE STORY OF THE MOVIE

PAUL HARRISON

SCHOLASTIC

Scholastic Children's Books
Euston House, 24 Eversholt Street,
London NW1 1DB, UK
A division of Scholastic Ltd
London – New York – Toronto – Sydney – Auckland
Mexico City – New Delhi – Hong Kong

First published in the UK by Scholastic Ltd, 2007

Editorial Director: Lisa Edwards
Project Manager: Neil Kelly
Project Editor: Laura Milne
Designer: Aja Bongiorno

Adapted from *The Golden Compass*™ movie screenplay by Paul Harrison

ISBN-10: 1 407 10320 2
ISBN-13: 978 1407 10320 4

2 4 6 8 10 9 7 5 3 1

Papers used by Scholastic Children's Books are made
from wood grown in sustainable forests.

www.scholastic.co.uk

$\mathcal{O}$ur universe is only
one of many. There are countless other
worlds, some of which look similar to our own,
but with amazing differences. In the world of
The Golden Compass, each person has a dæmon – a part
of their soul that lives on the outside of their body in the
form of an animal. The bond between human and dæmon is very
powerful – each feels the other's thoughts, emotions and pain.
A dæmon may change shape at will during childhood, but when a
person reaches adulthood the dæmon settles on a form.
This is the world of Lyra Belacqua, a twelve-year-old orphan who
lives under the protection of the scholars of Jordan College in
Oxford, Brytain. She was sent there by her stern uncle, the
explorer Lord Asriel, when she was very young. Lyra does
not realise it, but her life is about to change forever.
According to an ancient prophecy, she will decide
the fate not only of her own world, but
also that of all the worlds
in every universe...

Lyra crept down the dusty corridors of Jordan College, through the Dining Hall and towards the mysterious Retiring Room. She was in a curious mood, and had decided to investigate the special chamber used by the Jordan scholars. She wasn't allowed in the Retiring Room – which was reason enough for her wanting to see what it looked like. As always she was accompanied by her dæmon, Pantalaimon, or Pan for short. "Stop clomping about or we'll get caught for sure!" Pan whispered.

"They're making too much noise to hear from the kitchen," retorted Lyra. "Stop being a coward."

*P*an changed into a bird and flew into the Retiring Room with Lyra. They didn't get long to look around; at the sound of footsteps outside, they ducked into a wardrobe just as a servant entered carrying a decanter of wine. He was quickly followed by the Master of Jordan College and Fra Pavel from the Magisterium, the international organization that controlled day-to-day life in Lyra's world.

The Master and Pavel were talking about Lord Asriel and his new expedition.

"As Master of Jordan you must force him to abandon his plans," barked Pavel.

The Master would not agree. Asriel was a respected Fellow of the college; he would be allowed to do as he pleased.

Fra Pavel did not intend to take no for an answer. When the Master had gone, Pavel poured a white powder into the wine that had been left for Lord Asriel. Satisfied, he left.

"He's trying to poison Uncle Asriel," said Lyra, horrified.

"You don't know that," replied Pan, still thinking of the spanking they would receive if they were caught.

Any further discussion was swiftly abandoned when Lord Asriel himself strode into the room with his snow-leopard dæmon, Stelmaria. He poured himself some wine from the decanter and was about to take a drink when Lyra burst from the wardrobe and knocked the glass from his hand. Surprised and shocked, Asriel grabbed Lyra's wrist.

"It's poisoned!" she cried. "I saw the man from the Magisterium pour powder into it."

Asriel studied the decanter of wine, but there were footsteps approaching the room.

"Back in there," he said pushing Lyra and Pan back into the wardrobe.

The Master and Fellows entered the Retiring Room and sat down, waiting for Asriel's presentation. Pavel glanced to the floor and noticed the broken glass. Asriel switched on a large projector. A three-dimensional image appeared of a man and his dæmon surrounded by glowing particles.

"I went to the Arctic twelve months ago," Ariel said. "There I took this photogram at the magnetic North Pole in Svalbard. It isn't light that's coming down from the sky towards the man. It's Dust."

The Fellows
started to talk
excitedly to one another.
"What's Dust ?" Lyra
whispered to Pan. But her
dæmon didn't know.
"As you can see," said Asriel,
"the particles of Dust are flowing into
the man through his dæmon. I intend to travel to
the source of this Dust."

On the photogram image, the shimmering outline
of a city could be seen – suspended in the sky.
"A city in another world – a parallel universe, one
of many," Asriel continued. "From there and other
worlds Dust flows. I intend to travel there."

To Fra Pavel, the idea was scandalous. The Fellows
were astonished, and promised Asriel funding for his work.

Once the presentation was over and the coast was clear, Asriel pulled Lyra from the wardrobe and marched her across the college, ignoring her questions about what had just happened.

"Can I come with you? I want to learn about Dust and everything!" she said.

"What do you know about Dust?" Asriel snapped angrily.

"Nothing," replied Lyra.

"Good. Keep it that way, Dust is none of your business. If you're a good girl I'll bring you back a carved walrus tusk."

And without so much as a goodbye, he left.

That night, Lyra sat with her best friend Roger Parslow at their favourite meeting place – the roof of the college. They were talking about the mysterious Gobblers, a sinister group said to be responsible for the disappearance of children around Oxford.

"They're cannaboles," said Lyra. "They fatten you up and eat you."

"Roger," she continued, "I promise if you was taken by the Gobblers I would come and rescue you. You'd rescue me, too, wouldn't you?"

"Course I would. But everybody would go looking for you, you're a lady."

This was true; Asriel had sent Lyra to Jordan in the hope she would become refined. But Lyra certainly didn't like to be thought of as a lady, and fiercely denied Roger's claim.

Suddenly a servant's voice called from below: "Lyra! Come and get dressed! The Master wants you at High Table!"

With Lyra gone, a bored Roger tramped around the gardens. A rustling noise caught his attention.

"Lyra is that you?" he called. His dæmon, whose name was Salcilia, turned into a butterfly to investigate. Suddenly a monkey with beautiful golden fur appeared and grabbed Salcilia. A dark shape moved towards Roger. "Let us go!" he cried. But there was no one around to hear him.

Lyra sat, scrubbed and indignant, at the High Table in the Dining Hall. From the raised platform on which the table sat she could see rows of Fellows in the grand-looking room.

The Master was in the middle of lecturing Lyra on her poor attitude. "Lyra my dear," he said, "I know you do not always understand our wish to educate you, but sometimes you must do what others think best."

"I disagree Master." The voice stopped the Master dead. Standing there was a beautiful and commanding woman.

"Who's she?" whispered Pan to Lyra.

"Dunno," replied Lyra. "But she shut up the Master all right."

"Mrs Coulter," said the Master, "this is our Lyra. Lyra, Mrs Coulter. A ... friend of the college."

Mrs Coulter sat next to Lyra, and throughout the meal dazzled her with her tales of the Ice Bears of Svalbard, or the Panserbjørne as they were also known. She confided in Lyra, telling her how the king of the bears, Ragnar Sturlusson, wanted a dæmon as bears didn't have their own.

Lyra was totally smitten with the glamorous stranger. And then Mrs Coulter had an amazing idea.

"I'm going back to the North very soon," she said. "I shall need an assistant. Perhaps you should come."

Lyra was thrilled at the idea, but the Master looked concerned.

"I'm not sure that would be consistent with Lord Asriel's wishes for Lyra's education," he said.

"Let me deal with Lord Asriel," replied Mrs Coulter.

The Master looked defeated and agreed. Lyra was ecstatic at the prospect of spending more time with Mrs Coulter. But Pan was not so sure about Mrs Coulter's dæmon – a sleek monkey with golden fur...

As Lyra prepared to leave the next day she had an unexpected visitor – the Master. He looked agitated and was clutching a leather satchel.

"I ask of you a favour," said the Master, taking a small, compass-like object from the satchel.

"This is an alethiometer," he said, handing her the golden device. "It belonged to Lord Asriel. And now I am giving it to you. I feel you are meant to have it."

"What does it do?" asked Lyra.

"It tells the truth. I cannot teach you how it works, for the art is lost. But I must ask you – and this is of the utmost importance – that Mrs Coulter is never to know you have it."

Lyra, confused and troubled though she was by the request, left to join Mrs Coulter.

The Master and his fellow scholar, the Librarian, watched sadly as Lyra headed out of Jordan College.

"We have failed her," said the Master.

"We protected her as long as we could," countered the Librarian.

"Yes, but you know what the prophecies say," the Master replied.

"Surely you don't believe those old stories?" the Librarian asked incredulously.

Their discussion was abruptly halted as the door to the Retiring Room burst open. In marched Fra Pavel at the head of a squad of armed Magisterial guards.

"Master, I have a warrant for your arrest. The charge is heresy!" barked Pavel, furious at the Master for supporting Asriel's work. "Now, tell me where the alethiometer is."

The Master merely smiled.

Outside the college Lyra and Mrs Coulter prepared to board the sky ferry to London.

"Where's Roger?" Lyra asked.

"Who?" replied Mrs Coulter.

Lyra explained, but Mrs Coulter was in no mood to wait and hurried Lyra on to the ferry.

The sky ferry was a luxurious way to travel. At the front of the cabin Lyra and Pan sat in wonder, staring down at the impressive city below. Dominating the skyline was the Magisterial Seat, the London headquarters of the Magisterium.

After all her years in the relative quiet of Oxford, London felt very strange to Lyra. There were sky ferries droning overhead, tall buildings and bustling throngs of people. Even Mrs Coulter's home was pleasantly odd – as grand as any building in Jordan College, but at the same time inviting and cosy.

*L*yra's first few days in London were a whirl of activity, too. She was reeling from all the fine clothes Mrs Coulter bought her and the sophisticated dinner parties that they attended together. Most of all, it was the attention she received – something that had been lacking at Oxford – that really turned her head. But Pan was less than impressed.

"Likes to show off her new pet, doesn't she?" he said sarcastically.

"You just don't like her. Well, hard luck, because I like her," replied Lyra.

Despite Lyra's protest, she had not told Mrs Coulter about the alethiometer, and always carried it with her in its special leather satchel. She even kept it under her pillow at night for safe keeping.

Soon Lyra had the proof that all was not as it seemed. One night she and Mrs Coulter were discussing one of the guests they had met at a dinner party. Mrs Coulter explained that he was an expert on particle metaphysics.

"Have I explained what particles are?" she asked.

"You mean like Dust?" replied Lyra, showing off.

Suddenly the atmosphere changed.

"And what do you know of Dust?" asked Mrs Coulter coldly.

"That it comes from space," stammered Lyra.

"There are some subjects we don't speak about," replied Mrs Coulter firmly.

"But I didn't...." Lyra began.

"Yes, you did not know this so I forgive you. Now can you please take off that childish bag you always carry, I hate seeing you wear it indoors."

Lyra clutched the satchel close to her and refused.

"If you do not obey me," said Mrs Coulter, "we will have an argument, which I will win."

Mrs Coulter's dæmon – the Golden Monkey – grabbed hold of Pan and began to drag him further and further away from Lyra. This stretched the invisible, untouchable bond of energy that connected the girl and her dæmon, causing them both intense pain. Lyra had no choice but to put the bag down.

Having demonstrated her power, Mrs Coulter and her dæmon left.

*L*yra and Pan were furious with Mrs Coulter and the Golden Monkey. "I hate them both!" said Lyra. "Why do they want us here?"

That night, they crept downstairs and let themselves into Mrs Coulter's study. Lyra went straight to the desk and Pan searched the wastepaper basket. He found pages with lists of children's names. Next to each child's name was a "Dust count" and the words "candidate for intercision."

"And look at the name at the top of the forms," said Pan. "The General Oblation Board. The G.O.B...."

"Gobblers!" cried Lyra. The bottom of each page was signed by Mrs Coulter. "She's runnin' the Gobblers!"

Ref.
January ~ Mar
FILE 75/J
(with council ammend

CONFIDENTIAL

GENERAL OBLATION BOARD
Restricted Material

At that moment they heard Mrs Coulter's voice in the distance calling for Lyra. Quick as a flash, they dashed out of the room into the corridor, trying to look as innocent as possible. Mrs Coulter appeared in the doorway of the drawing room.

"Lyra dear," said Mrs Coulter, "what have you been doing?"

"Nothing," Lyra replied.

"Then come and help me," said Mrs Coulter beckoning her towards the drawing room. But then Lyra heard a noise coming from her own bedroom – Mrs Coulter had been trying to keep her distracted!

Lyra burst into her room and found the Golden Monkey holding the alethiometer. Pan changed into a bird, snatched the golden device from the Monkey's hand and flew through the window, followed swiftly by Lyra.

Lyra and Pan escaped into the night. They wandered the streets, trying to avoid the police. But they were being followed, and three dark figures chased them through the streets. Nets descended and Lyra and Pan were caught. Just when all seemed lost, a group of Gyptians appeared and overpowered their captors.

The Gyptians were tough warriors and traders. Lyra knew Ma Costa, the leader of her rescuers; she was the mother of Billy Costa – a friend of Lyra's in Oxford.

Ma Costa explained that they had been keeping a watch over Lyra ever since she left Jordan College. She and her family were going to meet up with John Faa, king of the Gyptians. He had called all the Gyptian tribes together to head north. They were looking for all the children kidnapped by the Gobblers.

Lyra accepted the Gyptians' offer to join them, and Ma Costa's barge slipped down the Thames. But on the other side of London, Mrs Coulter was still looking for Lyra. She suspected that Lyra was with the Gyptians, who had been spying on the Magisterium. Deciding to let a captured Gyptian spy escape, Mrs Coulter released two spy-flies – clockwork, insect-like tracking devices. Buzzing furiously, they flew into the sky.

Ma Costa's barge met up with John Faa's ship in the North Sea. Lyra was brought to the leader of the Gyptians and his wise counsellor, Farder Coram. Lyra showed them the alethiometer. Farder Coram studied the device intensely. It had many symbols around the edge of a compass-like dial. The alethiometer also had hands, like a clock, which were moved by small knobs to point to different symbols.

A needle, which spun slowly, gave the answer to the desired question. John Faa hoped that the alethiometer would tell him the whereabouts of his spies, who had disappeared a few days earlier. But Farder Coram did not know how to read the symbols.

"Please, may I try?" asked Lyra. She took the alethiometer and moved the hands. Nothing happened at first, but then the needle spun around the dial and pointed to the hourglass and skull – the symbol of death.

"I pray you read it wrong child," said John Faa.

Then he and Ma Costa confirmed Lyra's worst fears – the Gobblers had kidnapped both Billy Costa and Roger Parslow and were taking them to the North.

At that moment a badly injured Gyptian fell on to the deck. It was Jacob Huismans, the last of Faa's spies. He was dying, and he told them that the other spies were dead or captured. Lyra's reading of the alethiometer had been right. Within moments, the spy-flies arrived! They dived and struck with deadly stings, but the Gyptians, their dæmons and Pan were more than a match for them. Although one spy-fly escaped, they managed to capture the other in a metal tin, which was given to Lyra.

That night Lyra and Pan stood on the deck of John Faa's ship, the *Noorderlicht*, as it headed north. Suddenly, a silent, dark figure drifted down from above. Lyra gasped - it appeared to be a beautiful young woman. The figure spoke, but not out loud; Lyra heard the words in her mind.

"I am Serafina Pekkala, Clan Queen of the Witches of Lake Enara," she said. "Tell Farder Coram that the place he seeks is called Bolvangar, the place of fear. A regiment of Tartars with wolf-dæmons guard it. It is a week's march from Trollesund, on the coast of Norroway."

And as quietly as she had arrived, the graceful form of Serafina Pekkala flew off into the dark night.

$\mathcal{A}$cting on Lyra's information, the *Noorderlicht* edged its way towards Trollesund. When the ship docked, Lyra found a quiet spot so that she could practise reading the alethiometer. Interpreting the device's complex meanings seemed to come naturally to her.

"That's some mighty fine clockwork you got there."

Lyra looked up to see a tall, friendly looking man with long white hair standing in front of her.

"The name's Lee Scoresby," he said. "And this old girl," he said nodding to his hare-dæmon, "is Hester." Lyra introduced herself and Pan.

"Normally I work as an aeronaut," Scoresby continued, "but I'm here to help a friend in a spot of bother."

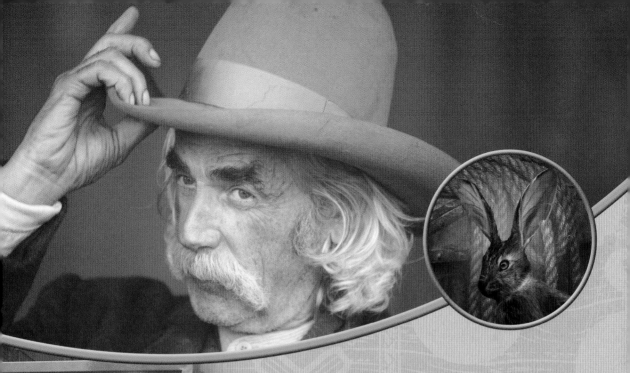

"Me too," replied Lyra. It was true — her friend Roger had been kidnapped and she was going to rescue him.

"Miss Lyra," said Lee. "I'd like to give you a word of advice. If I was on the sorta ...scout I reckon you're on, I'd hire me an aeronaut and an armoured bear. There's one in town. Iorek Byrnison's his name. Works at the sledge depot."

And he raised his hat and left.

That night Lyra and Farder Coram went looking for the armoured bear. They found him sitting behind a metal gate in a scrapyard near the sledge depot. Although the huge creature wasn't wearing armour, he was still a menacing sight.

The Ice Bear sat on his haunches tearing at a leg of reindeer meat, his white fur tinged with blood. Farder Coram and Lyra stayed close by the gate as Coram spoke to him.

"Iorek Byrnison, I offer you work."

"I have work," replied the bear.

"What kind of work is this for a Panserbjørne?"

"Paid work," replied Iorek, turning to collect a crock of whisky that had been left for him from the bar next door.

"Is that how they pay you?" asked Lyra. "With whisky?"

Farder Coram turned to leave. But as he was about to walk away, Lyra spoke up.

"Iorek Byrnison! I heard that bears live to hunt and to fight. Why are you wasting your time here?"

Iorek's powerful form bristled with fury.

"I stay because they gave me drink and then took away my armour while I slept. Without my armour ... I am nothing. It was no less than I deserved. I am an exile. I lost in single combat with another bear."

Iorek turned away, full of self-pity. Farder Coram again made to leave. As he did so, Lyra quickly checked the alethiometer and ran over to the Ice Bear.

"Your armour is in the Magisterium office," she said.

Iorek was amazed. "Then I owe you a debt," he said.

"I will serve your campaign until I am dead or you have victory."

Without a further word, Iorek charged off to retrieve his stolen armour.

Lyra chased after Iorek and found uproar in the centre of Trollesund. The doors to the Magisterium building had been ripped off and the Magisterial police were lining up outside. With a tremendous crash, an armoured Iorek burst out through the wall. Lyra ran to him and begged him not to fight.

"If you fight we'll never get away to rescue the kids!" she pleaded.

"Ready to fire!" cried the police captain, but he didn't get to finish the command to shoot. Lee Scoresby and the Gyptians had arrived. The police were outnumbered.

"Howdy Iorek," called Scoresby, pointing his revolver at the police captain. "I couldn't figure out how to spring you. Fortunately little girls come real resourceful down in these parts."

He turned to the police.

"What do you say you fellas just call it a day?"

Sensibly, the men from the Magisterium backed off.

With Iorek and Scoresby hired by the Gyptians, they all left Trollesund and spent the rest of the day trekking north. That night as they set up camp Lyra sought out the Ice Bear.

"The alethiometer tells me there is a hut on a lake in the next valley," she said. "It has something to do with the Gobblers. You could take me there." Iorek was surprised, but agreed to help.

With Lyra riding on the mighty bear they reached the mysterious hut in no time. It was a desolate and forbidding place.

"There is something not natural here," said Iorek, disturbed by the strange atmosphere.

Pan also felt oddly uncomfortable. When Lyra entered the ramshackle hut she found the reason. Huddling in the corner was a boy, distressed, frantic and alone – truly alone.

"Where's his dæmon?" asked Pan both horrified and disgusted.

The truth hit Lyra like a thunderbolt. "That's intercision! That's what the Gobblers are doing - they're cutting away kids' dæmons!"

Lyra managed to coax the boy from the hut. With a shock, she realised that it was her friend, Billy Costa. Iorek quickly carried Lyra and Billy back to the Gyptians. It was a bittersweet reunion for Ma Costa. Without his dæmon, her son seemed less than half a child and he didn't even recognise his mother.

There was little time to dwell on the reality of what was happening to the kidnapped children. Arrows whistled through the air as the camp came under attack. The Gyptians, caught by surprise, didn't notice Lyra being bundled on to a sledge and driven off.

The sledge sped through the night until it reached
a compound of low buildings behind a high,
wire fence. Lyra was escorted into a
bright entrance hall. It soon became
apparent that the officials had no
idea who she was.

"What is this place?" she asked
one of the officials.

"You'll like it," he replied.
"It's called the Experimental
Station. Lucky for you those
Samoyed hunters found you
wandering and brought you to us."

"I wasn't lost, there was
fighting," replied Lyra.

"Oh, I don't think so. Often, in the cold, you fall asleep and have bad dreams and you can't remember what's true and what isn't," said the official.

"What do you do here?" asked Lyra.

"We help children grow up," he replied pleasantly.

The official excused himself and Lyra was escorted to the canteen for dinner.

$\mathcal{L}$yra walked into the canteen — and immediately saw Roger! A quick look from Lyra told him not to react to her presence and she went to sit next to him.

"I knew you'd come," he said, overjoyed to see her.

"I promised, didn't I?" she replied. "I've come to rescue you with the Gyptians; but I need somewhere quiet to find when they'll get here."

$\mathcal{R}$oger and Lyra slipped out of the canteen and headed for a small dining room. Lyra went into the room and took out the alethiometer, while Roger waited in the corridor outside.

"That's strange," Lyra said to Pan. "The only thing the alethiometer says is that we shouldn't let Mrs Coulter get hold of it or we'll all die."

At that moment, a familiar voice rang out, striking fear into Lyra's heart. It was Mrs Coulter!

"Just how did several children wander free from the station?" said Mrs Coulter, who was standing outside in the corridor with two Bolvangar officials. There was no sign of Roger; he had disappeared when he heard people approaching. Lyra just had time to hide under the dining-room table before Mrs Coulter and the officials entered.

"Anyway," continued Mrs Coulter. "I have some good news. Lord Asriel has been arrested for heresy. He's being held in Svalbard by the king of the bears."

Lyra and Pan looked at each other in mute horror – Lord Asriel was a prisoner!

Mrs Coulter announced that she was tired from her long journey, and left the room to go to bed. Lyra breathed a sigh of relief, but then accidentally bumped into the table. The noise alerted the officials, who promptly discovered her hiding place. Realising that Lyra had heard too much, they marched her out of the room. They led her into a gleaming white chamber that looked like an operating theatre. Lyra and Pan were placed inside separate compartments inside a strange, cage-like machine.

"Oh, stop the noise," said an orderly to the struggling Lyra, "you want to grow up don't you?"

"It's only a little cut," added a nurse.

A doctor turned a switch, and a glowing guillotine hummed into action above them. Now, clearly visible in the light from the device, were the threads of energy that linked Lyra and Pan; threads that were about to be cut!

"What is going on here?" Mrs Coulter's voice silenced the room. "And who is this ch... Lyra!"

It was the last thing Lyra heard before she fainted.

Lyra jolted awake in a panic. Had it all been a dream? Pan was still there ... but so was Mrs Coulter.

"No one's going to harm you, Lyra, darling," said Mrs Coulter in a soothing voice.

"But Roger ... and the other kids ... why do it to them? Why be so cruel?"

"It may seem cruel," Mrs Coulter continued, "but it's for their own good. Just a little cut and they'll be safe from Dust forever."

"I don't understand – what's so bad about Dust?" asked Lyra.

"Dust is evil," Mrs Coulter replied. "Long ago one of our ancestors defied the Authority and Dust came into the world. Since then we've been sick."

"Dust doesn't collect around children. It happens later on, when you reach puberty and your dæmon settles. Then Dust gives you all sorts of nasty thoughts and feelings. But one little snip stops this. And your dæmon doesn't die, it just becomes like your special pet."

Lyra looked warily at Mrs Coulter.

"There's something else, Lyra. Your mother didn't die. The truth is that she wasn't married to your father, and although she loved you very much, she wasn't allowed to keep you. But later, when she was strong enough to do something about it she went to Jordan College..."

"No!" said Lyra, horrified.

"Yes. I am your mother."

"Then who is my father?" asked Lyra.

The truth dawned on her; it was Lord Asriel!

"Now perhaps you could give me the alethiometer," asked Mrs Coulter.

Lyra pulled out the tin that held the captured spy-fly. Mrs Coulter prised it open – and the spy-fly instantly attacked her dæmon. "Run Pan!" Lyra shouted.

Lyra and Pan sprinted down a corridor and halted briefly to set off a fire alarm. As she hoped, the children emerged sleepily from their dormitories to see what the noise was about.

"Come on!" she shouted.

They ran through the operating theatre, but Lyra paused as the children streamed past. The guillotine had to be destroyed. She lifted a recording machine from a desk and hurled it at the guillotine. The hateful device exploded in a shower of sparks, and Lyra ran from the operating theatre after the fleeing children.

The children poured
out into the cold night,
ignoring the shouts of
the adults pursuing them.
Then they heard a more
terrifying noise – the howls
of the Tartar guards' wolf-
dæmons. The sound stopped the
children in their tracks. Petrified, they
were surrounded by the Tartars and their
wolves. Defiantly, Lyra approached them.

"Go on then!" she shouted.

A wolf was released and leapt at her, but it was batted
out of the air by a massive paw – Iorek had arrived! With a snarl he
charged at the Tartars, who split into two groups; one to fight Iorek, the other
to deal with the children. The Tartars took up firing positions, but the order to
shoot never came. From above, witches swooped down, firing arrows at them.
And below, the Gyptians – led by John Faa – opened fire on the vicious guards.
The children were soon safely under the protection of the Gyptians.

A Tartar ran at Lyra and Roger, but he was felled by a shot from above. They looked up to see Lee Scoresby – with a smoking gun in his hand – descending from the sky in his airship.

"Miss Lyra! You said you wanted to fly, didn't you?" he called.

Lyra was determined to reach Svalbard and rescue Lord Asriel. Together with Iorek and Roger, she climbed aboard the airship and they took off, heading north towards the kingdom of the Ice Bears.

As the airship headed towards Svalbard, Lee Scoresby chatted to Serafina, who had flown alongside them. She sat on the edge of the airship's hull, while Lyra, Roger and Iorek slept below-decks. The Witch Queen told Lee about a prophecy which foretold that Lyra would decide the outcome of a forthcoming war.

"What would this war be about?" asked Scoresby.

"The Magisterium seek to control everyone in this and every other world," she replied. "They have been unable to extend their mastery, but if there is a way to travel between worlds, nothing will stop them. Nothing but us — and that child."

Suddenly a heavy snow squall hit the airship and everyone was shaken awake. Another strong wind tilted the craft and Lyra lost her footing. In desperation she reached out for Scoresby, but before he could grasp her hand, she tumbled over the edge. Fortunately, the soft snow broke Lyra's fall. Looking around at the bleak, white landscape, they realised that they were now hopelessly lost.

Two huge shapes loomed towards them out of the snow – Panserbjørne!

"You are a prisoner, come with us," barked one of the bears.

The bears took Lyra and Pan to the palace of the bear-king, Ragnar Sturlusson.

"Don't worry," said Pan, "Iorek will come."

"But they'll kill him before he even gets close!" Lyra replied grimly.

$\mathcal{R}$agnar's palace was a curious building, created from a combination of ice sculptures and stone. Heavily armoured Panserbjørne patrolled the battlements and guarded the corridors. Lyra and Pan were taken into an enormous hall, spattered with blood, seal skeletons and gull-droppings, where their ferocious captors presented them to the king of the Ice Bears.

Ragnar was even bigger than Iorek. His massive, powerful form was grandly attired in jewels, and his claws were gilded with gold. He looked at Lyra with cunning eyes. Sitting on Ragnar's knee was a human-shaped doll.

Suddenly Lyra remembered Mrs Coulter telling her how Ragnar wanted his own dæmon above anything else – the doll must be a substitute for a real dæmon! This gave Lyra an idea.

"Greetings great king!" cried Lyra. "And who are you?" growled Ragnar.

"Iorek Byrnison's dæmon," replied Lyra. Ragnar was both astonished and enraged. Lyra's trap had been set – and the bear-king was about to fall into it.

"I want to be your dæmon, not his," said Lyra. "He's just an exile, but you are better in every way. He's on his way now to fight you. If you defeat him, great king, I will become your dæmon. But you must kill Iorek in single combat."

Ragnar thought for a moment. He had beaten Iorek once – now he could finish him off forever.

"Yes!" he cried. And then he did something very strange for a bear – he smiled.

$\mathcal{I}$t was only a matter of time before Iorek appeared, carrying Roger on his back. Lyra was worried that she had done the wrong thing, and told Iorek about her plan. But she knew that this was Iorek's only chance – the Ice Bears would have killed him on sight if she hadn't set up the duel.

"I shall call you Lyra Silvertongue. To fight him is all I want," replied Iorek.

Ragnar waited at the combat ground, outside the palace gate. Panserbjørne circled around, eager for the fight to begin. Ragnar and Iorek roared at each other and it began – a brutal and terrifying sight. The two great warriors traded furious blows, speckling the snow with blood, but Iorek was coming off worse. His left forepaw appeared to be damaged, and he could only launch weak strikes with his right forepaw. Blow after blow rained down on Iorek as he tried to shield himself from Ragnar's savage attacks.

"Is that all?" cried Ragnar, triumphantly.

But Iorek wasn't as badly wounded as he appeared. He was playing for time, using human-like cunning to outwit his vain and foolish enemy. Iorek found a firm grip on the icy floor and launched himself at Ragnar. With a ferocious swipe of his left forepaw, he slashed out at his old adversary. Within moments it was over, and Ragnar's dead body fell limply on to the ice.

"Yes. That is all," said Iorek. He turned to the watching Panserbjørne.

"Bears – who is your king?" he cried.

They replied as one: "Iorek Byrnison!"

With Iorek's position as the new king of the
Panserbjørne secured, Lyra and Roger went off in
search of Lord Asriel. A sentry bear led them to the
prisoner's ward. He heaved open a rough metal
door, but the door didn't open on to a
cold, barren prison cell. Asriel's quarters were
luxurious, with expensive chairs, desks and carpets.
A roaring fire flickered away in the corner.
On seeing Lyra, Asriel looked horrified.
"No! Get out! I did not send for you!" he cried.
Then he saw Roger, and composed himself.
Lyra introduced her friend. Asriel listened
patiently, then summoned his butler to show
Roger to a bedroom so he could get some sleep.

"Lyra, sit with me awhile," said Asriel.

"I don't understand," said Lyra, looking around Asriel's comfortable quarters. "I thought you were a prisoner."

Asriel told her that Ragnar had thought it wise for him to continue his studies into Dust. He explained that Dust linked people and their dæmons. When this link was broken, it released a great amount of energy.

"But what is it?" asked Lyra.

"Dust? Well, that's just what I'm going up there to find out."

He paused. "You have brought me the one thing I need. Now rest." Asriel took Lyra to the room where Roger was already sleeping. Confused and exhausted, Lyra settled down to sleep.

A while later, Lyra woke with a start. Not only was Roger's bed empty, but there was also no sign of Asriel — and his quarters had been hurriedly cleared.

Lyra quickly checked her alethiometer and was shocked by what it told her. She called for Iorek, and climbed up on to his back. They pounded across the ice and soon caught sight of Lord Asriel and Roger.

"The alethiometer says he'll hurt Roger," Lyra told Iorek.

But as they got closer the ice beneath became too thin to hold Iorek's weight. Lyra had to go on alone. Tearfully she said goodbye, then crossed a narrow bridge of ice and headed off in pursuit of Asriel and Roger.

Lyra climbed over an icy ridge just in time to see Asriel starting up a strange machine. Roger was connected to it by a thin cable. The machine began to hum with energy, and suddenly Roger's dæmon exploded in a vivid burst of light. A bolt of energy fired up into the air, creating a huge opening in the sky – a gateway to other worlds.

$\mathcal{L}$yra raced towards Asriel's machine, but Roger was gone. A voice rang out, echoing across the icy landscape. Lyra turned around, and to her surprise saw Mrs Coulter walking towards Asriel across the ice.

"What have you done?" she asked, gazing up at the hole in the sky.

Mrs Coulter approached Asriel, warily. Suddenly he embraced her and they kissed passionately. "Will you come with me, Marisa?" he said.

"I daren't," she replied. Asriel turned to Lyra.

"You wanted to see the North? You wanted to learn about Dust? Now you can." he said.

"Not with you!" cried Lyra. "How could you do that to Roger?"

"You have no idea what's at stake," replied Asriel. "One child doesn't matter." Then he walked into the light and disappeared.

The ice around Lyra and Mrs Coulter was starting to break up.

"Come Lyra," said Mrs Coulter.

"No. You don't deserve me," replied Lyra.

The ice on which Mrs Coulter was standing broke off and she drifted away. Then Lyra noticed that the alethiometer – which had fallen out of her coat on to the ground – was surrounded by glowing particles of Dust. Suddenly the needle began to spin around.

"Pan!" said Lyra. "What if Dust isn't just power, or evil? What if Dust is alive ... and good?" She picked up the alethiometer.

"It says I know the way." The hole in the sky was getting bigger – and through it Lyra could see the ghostly outline of a huge city.

"Come on Pan, we'll follow the Dust. We'll learn about it, and we'll bring Roger back! And when we find him, we'll know what to do."

Together, they walked into the glowing gateway – and into a different world.